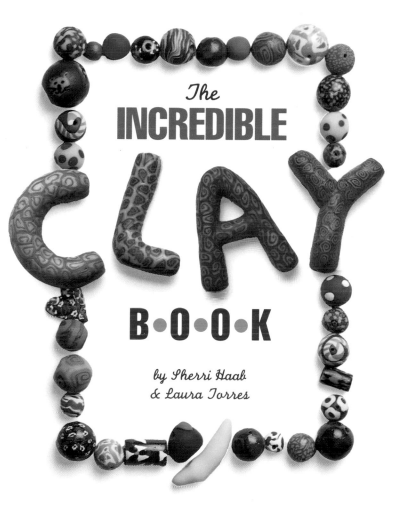

The INCREDIBLE CLAY B•O•O•K

by Sherri Haab
& Laura Torres

Klutz Press ● Palo Alto, California

Design and Art Direction:
MaryEllen Podgorski
Photography: Peter Fox
Graphic Production: MaryEllen Podgorski
and Eileen Stolee
Sourcing and Manufacturing: DeWitt Durham
Constant Meddling: John Cassidy

Book manufactured in Singapore.
Clay manufactured by Polyform Products,
Schiller Park, Illinois.

Write Us.
Klutz Press is an independent publisher
located in Palo Alto, California and staffed
entirely by real human beings. We would
love to hear your comments regarding this
or any of our books.

If you are having trouble locating additional
copies of this or other Klutz books, give us a
call at (415) 857-0888 for the name of your
nearest Klutz retailer. Should they be tragi-
cally out of stock, additional books and
additional clay can be ordered from our mail
order catalogue. See back page.

Klutz Press
2121 Staunton Court
Palo Alto, CA 94306

ISBN 1-878257-73-0

4 1 5 8 5 7 0

Contents

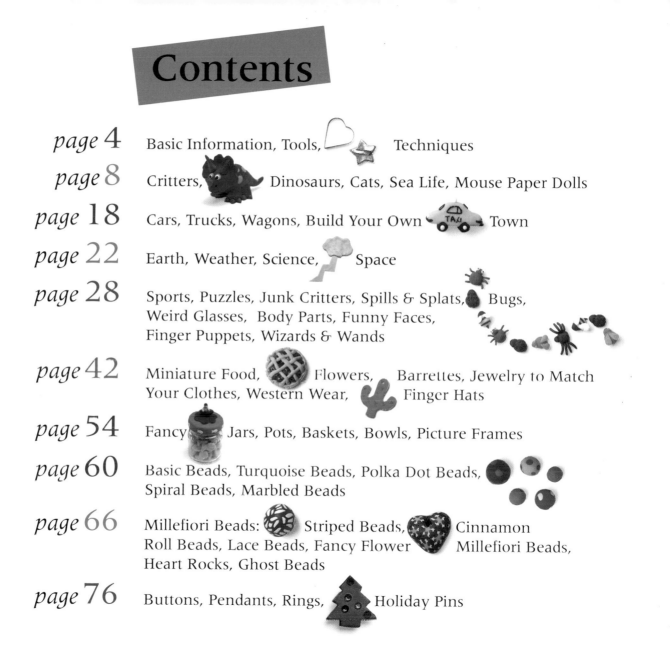

Basic Clay Information

What Kind of Clay Is This?

e made all the beads, buttons and other goodies pictured in this book with a new kind of clay that's officially known as a "polymer clay," since it's man-made rather than dug from the ground. If you've bought this book, you now own eight ounces of it— the very same kind we used.

Recently, polymer clay (you can buy more from us or at a craft or hobby shop) has become very popular for a number of good reasons:

- It bakes in a normal oven easily, permanently and unshrinkably
- It comes in a rainbow of colors
- It's non-toxic, clean and unmessy
- It's easy to work and shape

Does It ry Out or Harden?

Not really, although we recommend you store it in something airtight and away from direct sunlight. If you forget and leave the lid off though, it shouldn't be any problem. It's not like Play Dough.

The clay can get a little stiff in cold rooms, and a little soft in hot ones. If it gets stiff, just work it between your hands. If you've got the opposite problem just stick it in the refrigerator until it feels better.

Does It Stain?

You could probably stain something if you really worked at mushing the clay into it. It's not nearly as dangerous as paint, though. If you get clay on the carpet or your clothes, wash with warm soap and water. We clean our hands with baby wipes between colors, and we work on a clean surface so the clay doesn't pick up a lot of dirt — which it will, given the chance.

Can It Ruin My OveN?

No. If you fall asleep and completely burn your clay to a crisp— stinky fumes will come and you will know it. Don't stand there and breathe them deeply. Open the oven and windows and air the kitchen and stove out thoroughly. Once that's completely done, you can pop the dinner in fearlessly. (And next time, set a timer.)

Polymer clay has been certified for compliance with ASTM D-4236 by the Art & Craft Materials Institute. It's non-toxic, but don't eat it.

Basic Techniques

The Two Biggest Secrets

1. A little goes a long way. Work small. Cut off little pieces — sometimes tiny pieces. The eight ounces here should make at least a couple dozen creations — but only if you work at the right size! Roll the crumbs together when you're done and mush them together for re-use.

2. Think of each creation as a "clay kit." Many of the creations here are like little potato people. Form a basic shape, make little parts to go on it, then stick them all together (for which a toothpick is very handy). A face might look complicated until you break it down into its parts: the hair is just ropes, the eyes are little disks, the nose a triangle, and the lips red hearts. Make the simple parts — and stick them together.

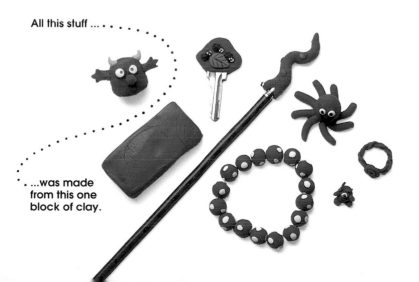

All this stuff ...

...was made from this one block of clay.

How to Bake

Do NOT use a microwave oven.

DO use a grown-up assistant.

Put your creation on a glass baking dish. Wash the pan thoroughly after use.

Heat your oven to 275 degrees. Exactly.

Bake 10 to 15 minutes for small objects. Large objects usually take 15 to 30 minutes.

Let cool completely before you try to take your objects off the pan. This takes patience, but you can break your creation if you don't wait. A little bit of sticking to the pan is normal.

If your oven runs hot or cold, your local oven expert will probably already know. But if you have to test, use a small blob of white clay. If it turns yellow before 10 to 15 minutes have gone by, your oven runs hot. Turn it down a bit. On the other hand, if your objects are quite breakable, your oven might be running cool. Try baking them a little longer.

Toos

A pair of hands is the only really essential tool. After that, a toothpick, a regular oven, and a glass baking dish or pie tin are all you really need for the basics.

For fancy shaping, or trickier creations, you might try using any of the following:

 Polymer clay requires special glue— the regular stuff just won't hold. Use E-6000 glue— you can buy it at craft and hobby shops, or from us.

 A basic. Good for poking holes or mushing two pieces of clay onto each other.

Basic cutting tool. Wash very thoroughly after use, or just make it into a "clay only" knife.

Use with grown-up assistant and for making fancy beads that need sharp cuts.

 Good for cutting out shapes.

 Good for rolling out sheets of clay. A drinking glass can also work.

Use in combination with the rolling pin to make flat sheets. Two magazines also work.

 Make wax paper your basic working surface. Tape it down on the table top. Also use it over clay when rolling.

Clayperson's Secret: Big things  are almost always built around a scrunched wad of aluminum foil. Saves clay and baking time.

ccessories for Your Junk Creations. Metal or glass things that can stand the heat of the oven can be baked right into the clay. Check with your grown-up assistant before baking anything (when in doubt— don't). Other things (plastic, paper, etc.) that can't be baked can be glued or stuck on afterwards.

Mixing Colors

This clay can be mixed exactly like paint. Any color you can imagine is available by blending these eight bricks. For a full blending, spend a little time working your chosen colors together completely and seamlessly. For a streaky, marble-like look, stop midway.

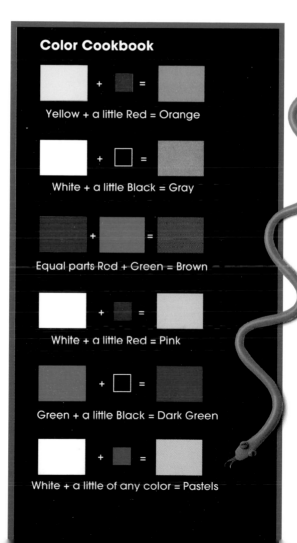

Color Cookbook

Yellow + a little Red = Orange

White + a little Black = Gray

Equal parts Red + Green = Brown

White + a little Red = Pink

Green + a little Black = Dark Green

White + a little of any color = Pastels

Shaping

Most everything in this book is made from three basic shapes put together in a million different ways:

Balls. Roll between your palms.

Logs. A rough log (or rope) can be rolled between your palms. A better log can be made by rolling on your work surface with your hands.

Flat Sheets. Lay two rulers (or magazines) on top of a big sheet of wax paper like this. Put the clay blob between the rulers, cover with another sheet of wax paper, and use a rolling pin.

Critters

Porcupine

- HOW MUCH CLAY? 1/4 block
- BAKE: 25 minutes / 275°
- TOOLS: box of toothpicks

1 Start with a ball of brown clay the size of a large marble. Press it down slightly so it doesn't roll. Don't use foil in the middle of this one, or the quills won't stay in firmly.

2 Gently shape another ball into a head as shown. Add four small balls for feet.

3 Add two tiny triangles for ears, a small black ball for nose, and two tiny black balls (or seed beads) for eyes.

4 Stick toothpicks all over body to form quills.

Skunk

- HOW MUCH CLAY? 1/4 block
- BAKE: 25 minutes / 275°

You can make the skunk, and lots of other critters, the same way you made the porcupine. The skunk's body started with a black oval. For the white stripe, apply a thin piece of white clay and add a furry texture by pressing a toothpick into the stripe.

L O N G   D O G

- HOW MUCH CLAY? 1/4 block
- BAKE: 25 minutes / 275°

Start with a brown log and t a k e i t f r o m t h e r e.

Snake

● HOW MUCH CLAY? For a small snake, a marble-size ball;
for a large snake, 1/2 block.
● BAKE: 10 minutes for small snake, 20 minutes for large one / 275°

Snakes are one of the easiest things to make out of clay. Just roll a rope, flatten one end into a head, and add a few eyeballs. If you want to get fancy, add spots, stripes and other snakey patterns. For a striped snake like the one wiggling here, make ropes of different colors, twist them together, then roll into a single smooth, friendly snake.

For spots, flatten small balls into circles, press them onto your rope, and roll the rope gently to smooth.

9

Dino Saurs

Triceratops is made the same way as stegosaurus.

Stegosaurus

● HOW MUCH CLAY? 1/3 to 1/2 block
● BAKE: 30 minutes, due to thickness and size / 275°

1. Crumple a piece of aluminum foil into an oval.

2. Cover the lump of foil with a thick piece of green clay.

3. Smooth out the body shape and form the head and tail.

4. Make the other small pieces as shown and press them onto the body.

5. Form the mouth by pressing a butter knife into the face.

6. Bake.

Flatten tiny balls for toenails.

Four fat legs.

Flatten circles to make spots.

Eyes are just flattened circles of different colors.

Flat triangular spikes for back.

Small cone-shaped spikes for tail.

Pteranodon

- HOW MUCH CLAY?
1/3 to 1/4 block
- BAKE: 20 minutes / 275°

1. Start with a thick log of clay and shape the head and tail as shown.

2. Form wings out of flat pieces of clay. Press them onto the body and smooth out the joints with your fingers.

3. Add eyes made from flattened black and white balls.

4. If you want to hang your pteranodon, stick a wire into its back before baking.

Paint discarded eggshells to make prehistoric eggs for hatching baby dinosaurs.

11

Beware of CAT

- HOW MUCH CLAY? 1/4 block
- BAKE: 25 minutes / 275°

Roll out a flat sheet and cut out an oval. Shape letters from thin ropes of clay.

Flat Cats

We rolled flat sheets of clay, cut out cat shapes and decorated them with bits of other colors.

pin

Jewelry

- HOW MUCH CLAY?
One large marble-size ball for a pin, one small marble-size ball for each earring.
- BAKE: 20 minutes for large items, 10-15 minutes for small.

Flatten balls for heads and bodies; decorate with bits of other colors. After baking, glue jewelry fittings to backs with E-6000 glue.

earrings

TO DECORATE A PAD

1. Roll a flat sheet.

2. Decorate it. (Our cat is just flat pieces— circles, pie slices plus a long pink skinny snake.)

3. Bake. Glue to the top of the pad.

Moonstruck Cat

- HOW MUCH CLAY? A large marble-size ball.
- BAKE: 15 minutes / 275°

Flatten a white ball into a circle. Cut out a silhouette cat shape.

12

The Corner Cat

- HOW MUCH CLAY? 1/4 block.
- BAKE: 20 minutes / 275°

1. Flatten a log into a strip as shown, and fold it over the corner of the frame.

2. Make body pieces as shown below. Press these onto your corner strip.

3. Refrigerate for half an hour so clay holds shape. Slide clay off frame and bake. When cool, attach to frame.

The Frame-Up (in Pieces)

Head is a flattened ball. Add triangles for ears; use smaller balls for facial features.

Flatten a log.

Teardrop shapes for paws.

Tail is a rope.

CAT HAT: Make letters from thin ropes. Cat faces are circles with triangle ears. Bake 10 minutes. Glue onto baseball cap with E-6000 glue.

Pocket Pals

- HOW MUCH CLAY? A large marble-size ball.
- BAKE: 15 minutes / 275°

Flatten a ball of clay for the face. Add ears and facial features. Make teardrop shapes for paws, curving them slightly forward. After baking, glue to a wooden tongue depressor or popsicle stick with E-6000 glue.

13

Striped Fish

- HOW MUCH CLAY? Small marble-size pieces of three different colors
- BAKE: 15-20 minutes / 275°

1. Trace a paper fish pattern and set it aside. Roll short skinny ropes of various colors and lay them side by side, touching.

2. Roll them into a flat sheet.

3. Place your paper pattern on top of the rolled clay and cut around it with a butter knife. Add seed bead eyes if you like.

P.S. For a **barrette**, glue a plain barrette onto the back of your fish after baking.

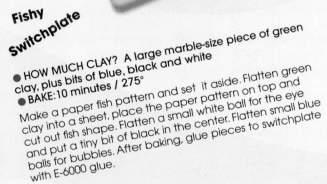

SEA LIFE

Fishy Switchplate

- HOW MUCH CLAY? A large marble-size piece of green clay, plus bits of blue, black and white
- BAKE: 10 minutes / 275°

Make a paper fish pattern and set it aside. Flatten green clay into a sheet, place the paper pattern on top and cut out fish shape. Flatten a small white ball for the eye and put a tiny bit of black in the center. Flatten small blue balls for bubbles. After baking, glue pieces to switchplate with E-6000 glue.

WAVES:

1. Roll ropes of blue and white clay. Twist them together and smush them until your get a swirly marbleized pattern—don't oversmush!

2. Roll out your marbleized clay into a flat sheet. Use a ruler as a guide to cut straight strips, then cut the top edge of each strip into wavy curves. Bake 25 minutes.

OCTOPUS:

Scrunch a wad of foil for the body base, then cover it with blue clay. Eyes are flattened white balls with smaller black ball in the middle. Stick on eight ropes for tentacles, and curve them around the toothbrush case. Gently slide the octopus off the case and bake for 30 minutes. When it cools, glue it to the case with E-6000 glue.

OYSTER:

Flatten two gray balls and shape them into top and bottom shells. Line the bottom shell with a thin layer of pink clay. Pinch the two shells together at the back and tuck a small white ball inside as a pearl. Bake 20 minutes / 275°.

Small fish are cut from
flat pieces of clay. Bake
10 minutes / 275°.

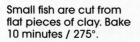

Fish eyes: Tiny black ball
or seed bead on a small
flattened white ball.

Press lines into
tail with a
toothpick.

Anchor is
shaped from
black ropes.
Bake 15
minutes / 275°.

MoUse Paper Dolls

● HOW MUCH CLAY? 1/2 block for mouse; for clothes, marble-size pieces plus bits of other colors
● BAKE: 20 minutes / 275°
● TOOLS: paper, scissors, waxed paper, rolling pin, two rulers, butter knife, toothpick, aluminum foil

MOUSE:

1. Trace the mouse pattern onto a piece of paper and cut it out.

2. Place two rulers a few inches apart on a sheet of waxed paper. Put a lump of gray clay between the rulers and cover with a second sheet of waxed paper. Use the rolling pin to roll out a flat sheet of gray clay.

3. Remove the top sheet of waxed paper. Place your pattern on top of the clay and cut around it with the knife.

4. Add features to the mouse and bake.

Trace me.

Nose and mouth: two gray balls dotted with a toothpick, a pink triangle and small black ball

Eyes: curve two skinny black ropes

Ears and paw pads: flattened pink balls

OVERALLS:

1. Roll out a flat sheet of blue clay and set the mouse on top of it. Trace around the mouse LIGHTLY with a toothpick. Add little tabs above the shoulders. Remove the mouse and cut out overalls with a butter knife.

2. Decorate the overalls as shown: Add a pocket and a red clay handkerchief, and prick "stitching" lines with a toothpick.

3. Squish a small piece of foil into a log. Curve the shoulder tabs of the overalls gently over the foil log and bake.

4. Make other clothes in the same way. To dress your mouse, rest the curved tabs on the mouse's shoulders.

How to Make a Real Rolling Wagon

● HOW MUCH CLAY? 1 block of red, plus a little black.
● BAKE: 25 minutes / 275°
You will need two pairs of store-bought wheels on axles. Hobby and model shops have them.

Roll out a flat red sheet and cut a rectangular base about matchbox size. Cut four strips and use them to build the sides of the wagon. Shape a black rope into the handle. After baking, glue the axles to the bottom as shown, using E-6000 glue.

How to Make a Keychain

● HOW MUCH CLAY? A large marble-size ball, plus bits of other colors.
● BAKE: 15 minutes / 275°

Roll a flat sheet and cut a rectangle. Decorate it with other colored shapes. (We made a sailboat out of a flat triangle.) You can shape letters with thin ropes. Before baking, poke a hole in one corner to attach the keyring.

Press a thin layer of clay over the top of a key and decorate it with other shapes. Be sure clay doesn't cover teeth of key! Bake 15 minutes / 275°

Truck in Bits

● HOW MUCH CLAY? a marble-size ball, plus bits of colors
● BAKE: 20 minutes / 275°

Shape trailer from a log of clay. Make other pieces as shown; stick them all together.

Front view

Superperson

Use blue logs for body, arms and legs. Pinch ends of legs to form feet. Bend arms at elbow, and add two tan balls for hands— place hands on hips for that superhero stance. Add a tan ball for head, a tiny ball for nose and a short log for neck. Use a rolled-out sheet of purple for a cape, and form the supernice logo by squashing a small green ball and adding thin yellow ropes for the letter. Bake 15 minutes / 275°.

For a building, roll out a flat sheet of clay and wrap it around a small cardboard box (we used an empty kitchen match box). Roll thin ropes to form windows.

Family Drive

Bodies of little people are tiny teardrops with balls stuck on for heads. Add teeny-weeny bits of clay for features, a coil for the high hairdo on Mom and a flattened ball with curled-up brim for Dad's hat. Press into car for fit, then carefully remove them and bake 10 minutes / 275°. Glue into car after baking.

Motorcycle Dudes

Shape basic body of animal and press lightly onto motorcycle. Add arms and legs and position correctly. Now add the other features; don't forget the helmet! Gently remove from motorcycle and bake 10 minutes / 275°. Glue onto motorcycle after baking. Vrroooooom!!

Cat

Form body from black logs; add tiny green eyes. Bake 10 minutes.

Trash Can Monster

Roll out a large flat sheet of gray. Cut out two circles, one for the bottom of the can and one slightly larger for the lid. Cut a long rectangle for the sides of the can and shape it around the bottom circle, pinching ends together— don't worry about making it perfectly round. Bend lid in a few places for that dented look and use gray ropes for handles. Monster is a green ball with long snaky fingers attached. Shape fingers around edge of can and gently remove. Bake separately for 15 minutes / 275°.

Tree

Make a wide-based trunk of brown clay. Bake 15 minutes. Then make small green balls and press them onto branches. Bake another 15 minutes / 275°.

Alien Construction Crew

Small chunks of gray clay for moon rocks. Each alien is a green log, split into three tentacles at the base. Use a tiny bit of yellow for hard hat. Stick alien driver into truck for position, then remove gently for baking. Bake 10 minutes / 275°.

Traffic Signs

Shape sign from bits of clay. Make a cone-shaped base. Stick a toothpick into base, then stick sign on top. Bake 10 minutes / 275°.

Fire Hydrant

Make a small red cone. Use small flattened balls for details; place a tiny one on top as a bolt. Bake 15 minutes / 275°.

Skateboard

Roll out a sheet of pink and cut skateboard shape. Flatten two skinny yellow ropes for stripes. Slightly flatten balls for wheels and add yellow centers. Curl up the end of the skateboard around a toothpick. Bake 15 minutes / 275°.

Mailbox

Start with a small gray rectangle for the bottom of the box. Make a slightly wider rectangle and arch it over the bottom; press along the edges. Make a gray door and red flag; press them on. Bake 10 minutes / 275°.

Slide

Use blue ropes for steps and a flat yellow rectangle for slide. Slightly curve the edges of the rectangle with your fingers or a toothpick. Bake 15 minutes / 275°.

Swing Set

Make purple logs for poles and squish together securely at joints. For swings, make blue rectangles with a hole at each end. Bake 15 minutes / 275°. After baking, use dental floss or heavy thread to hook up your swings.

The Earth

- HOW MUCH CLAY? 1 block of blue clay for base, assorted small pieces for details
- BAKE: 30 minutes / 275°

For the base, we rolled out one block of blue clay into a flat sheet and cut a circle by tracing around a saucer.

GLOBE PENDANT

Make a large marble-size ball of blue clay. Tear a few ragged pieces of green for continents and press them in place. Roll the ball gently to smooth it out. For a pendant, insert a thin piece of wire and bend it into a loop before baking for 20 minutes.

Thatch hut: Use brown cube for base of hut. Top with tan roof folded to make a triangle. Top with small brown cube for chimney.

Sandy beach: Texturize a flat piece of tan clay by pressing it against a piece of sandpaper.

Ocean: Press some small pieces of white clay into the blue base and smear them around to create surf.

Mountain: Pinch out a cone of gray clay. Cover the top with a smaller white cone, and texture with a toothpick.

Pine trees: Small cones of dark green clay.

Use a toothpick to scratch or press textures into the clay.

Leaves: Pinch tiny green balls into leaves.

River: Roll blue and white ropes and twist them together. Smush your twist until you get a streaky effect.

Boulders: Smooth, irregular chunks in various shades of gray.

Maps

● HOW MUCH CLAY? 1/2 block for a state, 1 block for a country
● BAKE: 25 minutes / 275°

1. Trace the shape of your favorite state or country from a map onto a sheet of paper and cut it out as your pattern.

2. Roll out a flat sheet of clay with a rolling pin. (See page 7.)

3. Place your pattern on top of the clay and cut around it.

To decorate the Lone Star State, we rolled out a flat sheet of blue clay and cut out a star with a cookie cutter, then cut a star out of Texas and fit the blue star into it.

Roll small marbles of clay into flat sheets and cut out shapes. Bake 15 minutes / 275°

SUN: Cut out a yellow circle, then roll some ropes. Pinch the ends of the ropes and curve to shape the rays, then attach all around the circle.

Charms

Make your shape a dainty size and poke a hole in top before baking. Bake 15 minutes. Attach the charm to your bracelet with a store-bought jump ring.

SNOWFLAKE: Roll out thin white ropes and press pieces together for snowflake.

For a refrigerator magnet, glue a small magnet to the back of the shape after baking.

24

Science Stuff

Germs

- HOW MUCH CLAY?
A small marble-size ball
- BAKE: 5 minutes /
275°

Make the germ's basic body by flattening a ball. Then add its special germy features using tiny ropes, balls, etc.

Mad Scientist

- HOW MUCH CLAY? 1/4 block
- BAKE: 15 minutes / 275°

Use a ball for the head and short log for the neck; blend seam with your finger. Shape ears and nose and attach them. Eyes are tiny bits of black. Skinny snakes form glasses, mouth, moustache and hair. Attach hair with a toothpick. Add a white log to base of neck and flatten on table top for balance. Press each end to form sloping shoulders. Bake.

Toe Life
(actual size)

Leaf Prints

- HOW MUCH CLAY? A large marble-size ball.
- BAKE: 15 minutes / 275°
- TOOLS: Waxed paper, rolling pin, a pretty leaf.

1. Set a ball of clay on a sheet of waxed paper.

2. Flatten the ball into a circle and place a leaf face down on top of it.

3. Cover with a second sheet of waxed paper and roll over it with a rolling pin.

4. Remove waxed paper and leaf, then bake.

Use this same technique for making prints of coins, lace, interesting buttons or anything else that has texture.

Rocket Science

Our intergalactic spacecraft are made by decorating small plastic flashlights. A mini-muffin tin is a useful mold.

1 Turn the muffin tin face down and cover two bumps with aluminum foil (this keeps the clay from sticking). Press two circles of clay down over two bumps.

2 Cut windows around the side of one clay piece. In the top of the other, cut a hole big enough to stick the flashlight through. Bake 20 minutes. When cool, remove clay from muffin tin. You will have two clay "cups."

3 Roll some ropes of contrast colors. Use one color to outline the windows. Place the second color around the rim of the other cup.

4 Press the wide rims of the two cups together. The soft clay rope on the second rim will work as mortar to hold the two pieces together. Bake 15 minutes.

5 Unscrew the flashlight. Glue the top of it inside the spaceship. Make sure no glue or clay covers screw threads of flashlight. Let the glue dry.

6 Screw on handle of flashlight.

Always make and bake decorations separately before gluing them onto anything made of plastic.

Flatten a ball of clay and make planet surface with a toothpick, pencil, etc.

Ink a rubber stamp and press it into a flat piece of clay.

Decorate a metal switchplate by covering it with a thin sheet of clay, then pressing on little designs. Bake 30 minutes / 275°.

Space Frame

● HOW MUCH CLAY? 1 or 2 blocks for frame, small bits for designs
● BAKE: 30 minutes / 275°

Decorate a picture frame using shapes cut from flat sheets, ropes, balls, etc. You can glue baked designs onto an existing picture frame— bake your decorations for 10 minutes, let them cool, then glue onto frame with E-6000 glue.

To make the frame, as we did here, roll out a large flat sheet of blue and cut a rectangle. Then cut an inner rectangle to fit your picture. Press your designs directly onto the unbaked frame— they will fuse during baking. Bake frame 30 minutes.

27

Sorts

SOCCER BALL: Roll a plain black ball. Cover all over with small flat black and white hexagons. Bake 15 minutes.

FOOTBALL: Start with a brown ball and shapes the ends into a football. Make four lengthwise creases with a knife. Decorate with thin white ropes. Bake 15 minutes.

SUMO WRESTLERS: Use a small marble-size piece of clay for each. Make body from balls and logs. Poke features and belly button with a toothpick. White triangle for trunks, black rope for hair. Bake 15 minutes.

PIN: Flatten a marble-size brown ball into a thick circle and cut out a glove shape. Flatten a smaller white ball and press onto the glove. Decorate the baseball with thin black lines. Bake 15 minutes. After baking, glue on a pin back using E-6000 glue.

BAT & BALL: Shape a bat from a tan log. Wrap a thin black rope around the handle. Press a white ball onto the bat; decorate the ball with thin black lines. Bake 15 minutes.

BOWL-O-RAMA: Poke toothpick holes in a black ball. Form a bowling pin out of a white log and decorate it with a thin red rope. Bake 15 minutes.

FIT MISS: Press pink logs together for arms, legs, and body. Add a pink ball head. Decorate with bits of clay for hair, facial features and leotard. Bake 20 minutes. Uses 1/2 block of clay.

28

The Puzzle

Page

● HOW MUCH CLAY?
1/2 block.
● BAKE: 20 minutes / 275°

Roll out a flat blue sheet
and cut out a fat **T** shape.
Make diagonal cuts
exactly as shown,
then bake.

Hand the loose
pieces to someone.
Tell them to make
a **T**. Guaranteed
to drive people
crazy.

● HOW MUCH CLAY?
1/4 block.
● BAKE: 20 minutes / 275°

Roll a flat sheet of clay and
cut out an elephant shape.
(Trace ours, if you like. Or,
use any cookie cutter to
make a different shape.)
Tusk is a pinched white
rope, eye is flattened balls.
Before baking, cut the
elephant into jigsaw pieces.

Tic Tac Toe

○ HOW MUCH CLAY? 1/2 block
○ BAKE: 25 minutes / 275°

Roll a thick flat sheet and cut out a
square. Roll thin ropes of another color
and crisscross them to make the grid.
Wrap a long flattened rope all around
as a border. Make **X** and **O** shapes out
of fat ropes; bake them separately from
the game board for
10 minutes.

Junk Critters

● HOW MUCH CLAY? A large marble-size piece for one critter
● BAKE: 20 minutes / 275°

You can make weird critters out of junk you have laying around the house. Cast a fresh eye on nuts, bolts, staples, pins, bottle caps, ... If you can bake it, you can use it! Start with a ball of clay, any color, to shape the body, then customize it with oven-proof junk. Don't use foil in the middle of these critters or the junk won't stay securely. Make sure you stick stuff in deep enough to stay.

Bottle cap and toothpick parasol, stuck together with a bit of clay; straight pin antennae and eyes; broken toothpick nose.

Make whale shape; cut slit for mouth; form tail. For eyeballs, mold clay around heads of straight pins and stick into head. Teeth are earring backs with the round part sunk deep into clay.

Staple hairdo, screw nose, staple eyelashes, coin feet.

Cut a slit for a mouth. Little metal balls for teeth. Screw feet, spring tail, snap and wire eyes stuck together with bits of clay and glue.

An old key makes a nice sawfish. Form clay around key for nose; shape the tail. Use a butterfly paper clip for a fin—cut off one triangle with wire cutters.

Cut a slit in a ball of clay for a mouth and add little metal pieces for teeth. Legs and eyes are electronic parts.

Use round balls for head, feet and body; eyepin jewelry findings for mane and face.

Use an old key for a guitar: Cover top of key and ends of teeth with clay; stick on straight pieces of wire for strings and foil stars for decoration. Use balls of clay for head and body, logs for feet and arms. Stick guitar onto body, then add arms. Foil star eyes, jacks for hair, wire necklace.

Balls of clay squished between bottle caps; foil arms and eyes; metal mouth.

Pig has a log body and legs, ball head, triangle ears. Seed bead eyes, tack nose, spring tail, penny in back. After baking, glue pig onto box with E-6000 glue.

For bird, stand a tapered log upright and form tail in back. Add tack feet, seed bead eyes, jump ring glasses, eyepin antennae. Wings are a butterfly paper clip cut with wire cutters; beak is a bolo tie tip. After baking, glue to box with E-6000 glue.

Zipper tab for tail, penny ears, straight pin nose, bits of wire for mouth and whiskers.

Cover the back of a large washer and leave an edge around the front for head; form a short body. Flatten balls for eye, thin ropes for eyelashes. Cut off pieces of paper clip (use a wire cutter) for mouth and nose.

Hair and feet are jacks sunk deep into clay. Seed beads for eyes and nose; wire mouth.

Start with a square of brown clay. Screen is a blue marble. Antenna is an open brad with the round part stuck into clay. Legs are brads stuck in with round parts showing for feet.

oOOOPS!

Banana Peel

● HOW MUCH CLAY? A large marble-size piece
● BAKE: 20 minutes / 275°

Roll out a flat sheet of yellow clay. Cut out three long peels and pinch them together at one end. Wrap a bit of brown clay around the top, and roll a few thin brown ropes for additional decoration. Arrange convincingly.

Get an empty milk bottle or carton. Press a very thin sheet of white clay into an irregular spill shape. Make a few small drops. Bake 15 minutes.

Splat!

Make bugs from small marble-size balls of clay, then squish 'em. Bake 10 minutes.

Empty and rinse a can of chocolate syrup. Press a thin sheet of brown clay into a realistic spill shape. Raise one end of the spill to "pour" out the spout. Bake 15 minutes. The ice cream is a ball of aluminum foil covered with pink clay. Use your fingers to spread out the bottom into a slight "melt." Bake for 25 minutes. Top with a real cone.

Bug Tacks

● HOW MUCH CLAY? Small marble-size ball
● BAKE: 10 minutes / 275°

Cover head of thumbtack with clay; decorate clay to look buggy. Push tacks into a wad of foil to bake.

Snowmelt

● HOW MUCH CLAY? 1/2 block of white, plus bits of colors
● BAKE: 20 minutes / 275°

Press down on a ball of white clay, spreading the bottom out with your fingers. Stick arms are made from black ropes; features are tiny balls. Bake.

Arrowhead

- HOW MUCH CLAY: One large marble-size piece each of red, blue and yellow, plus a wire coat hanger
- BAKE: 20 minutes / 275°

Cut and bend a wire coat hanger so the curve fits over your head. Shape the red clay into an arrowhead and attach it to one end. For the feathers, flatten the blue clay into shape; press in a texture with a toothpick. Roll a yellow rope, cut it in half, and squish it on to cover the straight parts of the

WIRE.

Bird Glasses

- HOW MUCH CLAY: 1/2 block of yellow clay and bits of other colors, a cheap pair of sunglasses and some feathers

For a nice chicken beak, roll out a flat yellow sheet and cut out a diamond about 2" x 2", and shape it into something beak-like (see photo). Then mold it to the glasses so it sticks. Chill in the refrigerator for 25 minutes so the beak shape will stay firm when pulled away from the glasses. Remove beak from glasses and bake it for 20 minutes / 275°.

For eyes, roll a flat sheet of green and cut two circles, then cut a smaller circle out of the center of each. Decorate each eye with radiating yellow ropes. Bake 15 minutes / 275°.

When cool, glue beak, eyes and feathers to glasses with E-6000 glue.

34

Weird GlAsses

- USES: Two marble-size pieces of white and one of green, plus a cheap pair of sunglasses
- BAKE: 10 minutes / 275° (The clay, not the sunglasses)

Flatten the two white balls into circles. Make two smaller green balls and flatten them too, then press one into the center of each white circle. After baking, glue the circles to the lenses of the glasses.

Fruit Fellers
& Ve**G**etable Volk

Face Pieces

Surround the head of a tack or nail with clay and use your imagination to make small facial features. Push the tacks into a wad of foil to bake them.

- HOW MUCH CLAY? Small marble-size piece
- BAKE: 10 minutes / 275°

FINGER HOOK

Make a log of flesh-colored clay and bend it into a hook shape as shown. Add realistic wrinkles and fingernail.

- HOW MUCH CLAY? 1/2 block
- BAKE: 25 minutes / 275°

Open-face sandwich.

Glue attachments to photos for that different look!

Make a flesh-colored log and poke your thumb into one end of it to form a snug-fitting hole. Lovingly fashion the log to resemble your own thumb on steroids.

- HOW MUCH CLAY? 1/2 block
- BAKE: 25 minutes / 275°

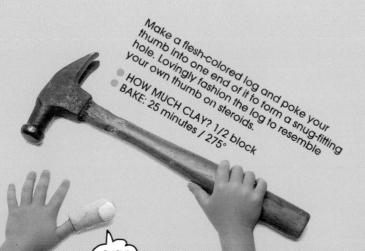

If you've been wanting an extra nose, a third eye, etc., now you know how to make one.

OUCH!

37

Funny Faces

● HOW MUCH CLAY?
Small marble-size ball,
plus tiny bits of colors
● BAKE: 15 minutes /
275°

Flatten a pink ball into a face.

Skinny yellow ropes.

Red bow with tiny white dots.

Nose.

Toothpick mark on lips.

Eyes: Flatten balls of clay: white on bottom, then a smaller black one, then a tiny white one on top.

Cheeks: Roll out tiny ropes of dark pink clay and coil them like a flat cinnamon roll.

Face: Flatten a marble-size ball of light blue clay.

Hair and eyebrows: Tiny purple ropes.

Red bow tie with white dots.

Skinny blue coils.

Skinny red rope curved into a circle.

Eyes: Tiny black dots on top of flattened white balls.

Spoon Family

● HOW MUCH CLAY? A large marble-size ball for each grown-up, small marble for each kid, plus bits of colors
● BAKE: 15 minutes / 275°

Smush a ball of clay over the back of <u>metal</u> spoon and press it to cover evenly. Make features from bits of clay.

Finger Puppets

● HOW MUCH CLAY? For each puppet, a large marble-size ball, plus small bits of other colors.
● BAKE: 25 minutes if dense and thick. / 275°

● TOOLS: Thimbles are optional. A garlic press is handy for Harry. Check with the grown-ups.

Alien appendages are ropes attached with a toothpick. Facial features are small balls, ropes and triangles.

Hairy Harry

1. Start with a ball of brown clay.

2. Stick your finger into the clay and shape the ball into a deep cap. Or shape around a thimble.

3. Clean your garlic press very thoroughly. Squeeze out a piece of brown clay to form the hair. Now wash the garlic press several times in soapy water to make sure it is really REALLY clean.

4. Flatten tiny balls to make eyes for your puppet. Attach the hair, starting with the bottom row and working up toward the crown of the head. A toothpick helps.

5. Bake the puppet. Take it off your finger first (bet you knew that).

Wizard

● USES: 1/2 block of purple, plus small bits of colors.
● BAKE: 25 minutes / 275°

This one takes a little time, but what do you expect? Wizards don't come easily.

Wizards, Wands and a FRog Prince

1 Squish aluminum foil into a cone.

2 Roll out a flat sheet of purple. Cut two triangles as shown for sleeves, and a curved rectangle for the robe. Decorate the hems with thin yellow ropes.

3 Wrap the rectangle around the foil cone to form the body. Roll the two triangles into sleeves and attach at the shoulders.

4 Roll a ball for the head; pinch out a nose and add two seed beads for eyes. For hands, make two teardrop shapes and press out fingers with a toothpick. For shoes, make two yellow teardrops and curl up the points.

5 Attach the head, hands and feet. Adjust the feet to make sure the body stands properly.

6 Find a marble to use as a crystal ball, and form a purple cone for the hat. Roll some thin white ropes for the beard.

7 Press the white ropes onto the head for hair and beard. Set the marble between the hands and press the hands around to hold it.

8 Put the hat on and decorate it with stars.

Castle

- HOW MUCH CLAY? 1/2 block
- BAKE: 25 minutes

Roll short gray logs and stand them together upright to form a castle with towers. Use a toothpick or pencil point to poke windows and ridges along the tops of the towers. Add a small brown square for the portcullis (look it up) and a piece of toothpick for a flagpole.

Star Wand

- HOW MUCH CLAY? 1/2 block
- BAKE: 20 minutes / 275°

Roll out a thick sheet of yellow clay and cut a star shape. Poke a wooden chopstick into the star as shown. Press in rhinestones or glass jewels if you have them, or decorate with other clay shapes. After baking, tie some pretty ribbons around the stem.

Sea Dragon

- HOW MUCH CLAY? 1/2 block
- BAKE: 25 minutes / 275°

Form dragon from green logs. Use a butter knife to press the mouth open; add a red forked tongue. Eyes and nostrils are tiny balls. Place triangular scales along back.

Power Rings

- HOW MUCH CLAY? A large marble of clay for each ring
- BAKE: 20 minutes / 275°

Flatten a small ball into a disk. (For a special power ring, wrap clay around a disk magnet.) Decorate. Roll a rope of clay and flatten it into a ribbon, then wrap it around your finger. Remove ring from your finger and press on the disk, then bake.

Crown is a flat yellow strip cut into points, then wrapped into a circle. Decorate with glass jewels, then bake.

Frog Prince

- HOW MUCH CLAY? 1/2 block
- BAKE: 20 minutes / 275°

Green ball for head; flatten it slightly, and press mouth line with a butter knife.

Press balls on for eyes.

Green ball for body.

Legs and toes are teardrop shapes pressed onto body.

For crown, cut one pointy edge on a flat yellow strip, then roll strip into a circle.

Sword in Stone

1. Fashion sword out of small balls of gray and yellow clay. Decorate with glass jewels and bake 10-15 minutes / 275°.

2. Press 1/2 block of light gray clay into irregular stone shape. Make a slit in it with a toothpick or knife. Test baked sword for fit. Bake stone 20 minutes / 275°.

Apple

1. Start with a ball of red clay and slightly lengthen the bottom.

2. Turn the ball over and press a few dimples with a toothpick.

3. Pinch small flat pieces of green to make leaves. Press in the center vein with a toothpick.

4. Attach the leaves and add a small brown stem.

Itty-bitty, teensie-weensie, little tiny,

Miniature F🫐🫐d

These all use bits of clay no bigger than a small marble.
BAKE: 10 minutes / 275°

Corn

1. Shape a yellow log and crosshatch it with a toothpick to mark kernels.

2. Form two flat pointy leaves and scratch a few lines into them with a toothpick.

3. Press the leaves around the ear of corn.

Watermelon

1. Make a ball of dark green clay and roll it slightly to make it oval.

2. Make skinny light green ropes and press them onto the melon. Roll the melon gently to flatten the stripes.

3. For the slice, decorate a pink triangle with two tiny black seeds. Press skinny ropes of white and green onto the base of the slice.

(twice actual size)

- Green pepper is made just like the apple.

- For a carrot, pinch one end of an orange log. Press a toothpick to form lines across the carrot. Add a few short green ropes at the top.

- For the banana, pinch the ends of a yellow log and curve them as shown. After baking, add a little brown paint.

- The orange is a ball pricked all over with a toothpick and topped with a tiny green leaf.

Peas

1. Flatten a narrow piece of green clay and pinch the ends as shown.

2. Make small green balls for peas.

3. Set the peas on the flat pod and fold up the sides to cradle the peas.

4. To make a tendril, wrap a thin green rope around a toothpick, then slide it off and attach it to the pod. Add a tiny leaf.

TINY TACO:

1. Flatten a tan ball into a circle and fold it over as shown.
2. Make tiny brown ovals for beans.
3. Flatten a very thin piece of green clay and tear it into lettuce leaves.
4. Roll tiny yellow ropes for cheese.

MICRO SALAD:

Lettuce is torn just as you did for the taco. Red wedges for tomatoes, orange ropes for carrots, black oval balls for olives—poke one end with a toothpick.

NOT MUCH SUNDAE:

For a fancy dish, flatten a blue ball into a circle and use a toothpick to press a scalloped edge. Three not-too-smooth balls for ice cream, draped with a thin piece of brown for syrup, topped with a cherry red ball.

SPAGHETTI FOR A SMALL PLANET:

1. Flatten a blue ball to make a plate.
2. Squeeze some white clay through a garlic press. Then clean the garlic press VERY thoroughly.
3. Add a flat red shape for sauce. Top with a few brown balls.

PEEWEE PIZZA:

Flatten a tan ball into a circle and press an indentation in the middle. Top with a thin flat red piece for sauce, some flattened brown balls for pepperoni and short thin white ropes for cheese.

TEENY WEINIES:

Cut a lengthwise slit in a tan log for the bun. Round off the ends of a red rope, place it in the middle of the bun and gently squeeze the sides of the bun. If you like mustard, top with a squiggly yellow rope. Bottles are shaped by pinching logs at the top and adding white labels and caps.

VERY TINY TURKEY:

Form a tan ball into an egg shape. Pinch log pieces into legs and wings and press in place.

LITTLE MAC:

Flatten balls into circles and stack them: tan bun on bottom, brown burger patty, green lettuce, red tomato. Leave the top bun slightly domed and add beige bits for sesame seeds.

(actual size)

FAKE BERRIES:

Roll a purple-black ball the size of a marble and cover it with small balls. Bake 15 minutes. For a glossy finish, coat with clear nail polish after baking.

LITTLE LOAVES:

The rolls are slightly flattened balls, pressed on top with a toothpick to make the **X**. Round the ends of a tan log to form a loaf of bread; press lines across the loaf with a toothpick. Bake all these for 5 minutes at 275°.

The cheese is a wedge of clay poked with a toothpick.

Pinch one end of a purple log to form the bottleneck. Cut a flat white square label and wrap a white cap around the top.

Continental Breakfast

CROISSANT:
Make a flat triangle. Roll the wide end of the triangle toward the point. Curve the roll into a crescent shape. Bake 5 minutes / 275°

CINNAMON ROLL:
Make two ropes of tan and brown clay. Place them side by side and roll into a flat coil. Bake 5 minutes / 275°

COOKIES:
Flatten tiny balls of brown and white clay into circles, then stack them to make sandwich cookies. Prick a design in the top with a toothpick. Bake 5 minutes.

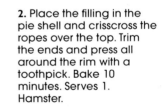

PIE:
1. Flatten a tan ball of clay into a circle and press an indentation in the center. Make small balls for the filling—red for cherries, purple for blackberries. Roll some thin tan ropes.

2. Place the filling in the pie shell and crisscross the ropes over the top. Trim the ends and press all around the rim with a toothpick. Bake 10 minutes. Serves 1. Hamster.

BIRTHDAY CAKE: Flatten brown and white balls into circles. Press irregular edges on the white circles. Stack alternating colors, ending with white on top. For the rosebud, coil a skinny pink rope. Pinch two small balls of green clay and crease with a toothpick to form leaves. Bake 10 minutes / 275°

LOW CHOLESTEROL BREAKFAST

For the frying pan, flatten a brown ball into a circle and add a strip all around to make the side. Attach a black log for a handle; use a toothpick to poke a hole in the end of the handle. For bacon, place ropes of tan and red side by side and flatten them into a ribbon. Set the ribbon into the frying pan, curving it a little.

The eggs are a flat blob of white topped with two flattened yellow balls. Bake 10 minutes at 275°. Yuck.

CRASH DIET COOKIES

Cover a small piece of thin cardboard with foil to make a cookie sheet. For cookies, flatten small tan balls and decorate with brown bits. Bake 5 minutes / 275°

FLOWERS

Bake all flowers about 15 minutes / 275°.

Camellia

1. Make a pink rope and flatten it slightly.

2. Starting at one end, fold the clay back and forth in a zigzag.

3. Shape it into a circle and pinch it together at the base.

For a larger flower, just make a bunch of these.

Rosebud

1. Roll a rope and flatten it slightly. Coil it like a cinnamon roll.

2. Flatten a small green ball and pinch one end into a teardrop shape.

Press veins into the leaf with a toothpick, then pinch base of leaf for a nicely curved base.

Tulip

1. Flatten three small balls and pinch them to form teardrops.

2. Place two teardrops as shown, then center the third one on top of them.

3. Use a knife or toothpick to score veins down the petals.

Two-Tone Rose

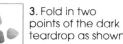

1. Flatten four small balls of pink clay and one dark pink ball.

2. Pinch each circle into a teardrop shape.

3. Fold in two points of the dark teardrop as shown.

4. Attach the light pink teardrops all around the center, pinching them at the bottom and curving out the top for a nice soft petal shape.

P.S. For a fuller rose, just keep adding more petals of slightly larger size.

Daisy

1. Flatten five tiny balls and shape them into teardrops.

2. Put teardrops in a circle with all their points touching at the center.

3. Flatten a small yellow ball for the center, then use a toothpick to press a line into each petal.

Fresh Bouquet Pin

- HOW MUCH CLAY? 1/4 block
- BAKE: 25 minutes / 275°

Roll out a flat sheet of clay and cut out a quarter circle 2-1/2" high.

2-1/2"

Roll the quarter circle into a cone shape— press the seams tightly and pinch the bottom to be sure there are no holes. The clay is waterproof but you have to make sure your container is watertight. After baking, glue a pin onto the back.

Watering Can

- HOW MUCH CLAY? A large marble-size ball, plus bits of colors
- BAKE: 15 minutes / 275°

Roll out a flat white sheet and cut out watering can shape. (You can trace this photo if you like.) Make tiny flowers for decorations and add thin blue ropes at rim and bottom. Make the dot border by poking with a toothpick.

After baking, glue on a pin back with E-6000 glue.

Strawberry Barrette

● HOW MUCH CLAY? Small marble-size pieces of green and red, bits of white
● BAKE: 20 minutes / 275°

1. Cover a small metal barrette with a strip of green clay.

2. Roll three red balls and shape the ends slightly to look like strawberries. Press them onto barrette.

3. Make a few green leaf shapes and press them next to the berries.

4. Poke holes all over the berries with a toothpick.

5. Make a few small white flowers. Stick them in the center to secure them to the barrette.

6. Place metal barrette right on the baking dish and bake.

7. When cool, coat with clear nail polish for shine.

8. For added strength, pop the clay decoration off the barrette and glue it back onto the metal with E-6000 glue.

Rose Barrette

● HOW MUCH CLAY? A small marble-size piece for each rose, two small marbles of green (one for leaves, one for base)
● BAKE: 20 minutes / 275°

I. Cover a metal barrette with a strip of green clay.

2. Make roses (page 47). Make a slightly larger rose for the middle of the barrette.

3. You can pre-bake the roses for 10 minutes, then press them onto the barrette. Make a few green leaves for support.

4. Bake 20 minutes on the barrette.

5. You can pop the clay design off the barrette and glue it back on with E-6000 glue to make sure it really sticks.

You can also try gluing your roses onto a bow.

Bows, Earrings, Necklaces

(and all that kind of thing)

Fruit Bow

Flatten small green balls and shape them into teardrops for leaves. Press veins with a toothpick. Make tiny fruit (like the necklace at left), press them onto the leaf cluster and bake 15 minutes at 275°. Glue onto a bow with E-6000 glue.

Fruit Salad Necklace

Form tiny fruits as shown below. Pierce a hole in each piece, then bake on a wire for 15 minutes. After baking, string the pieces on a cord, making a knot between each bead.

- *Banana* is a yellow log pinched at each end.
- *Orange* is a ball pricked all over with a toothpick.
- *Apple* is shaped from a red ball. Poke top with a toothpick and add a tiny green leaf.
- *Grapes* are a cluster of tiny purple balls, topped with green leaves.

eye pin finding

ear wire

Grape Earrings

Press small purple balls into a cluster. Add a grape leaf cut from a flat piece of green clay. Insert an eye pin finding into the top of each earring and bake 15 minutes at 275° on a wire, same as for beads. After baking, hook clusters to ear wires.

Hair DooDads

- HOW MUCH CLAY? A large marble-size ball for each, plus bits of colors
- BAKE: 15-20 minutes / 275°

1. Make head by flattening a ball of clay into a circle then adding ears, eyes, etc. with dots and tiny ropes.

2. The striped border on the cat is made with two ropes of contrasting colors twisted together then pressed all around the edge of the head.

3. Bake, then glue onto a ponytail holder or barrette with E-6000 glue.

Jewelry to Match Your Clothes

1. First, look at the designs and shapes in your fabric. Pick out some part that you like and make a paper pattern of it.

2. Roll out a flat sheet of clay and position your pattern. Cut out your shape with a knife. Add details and color with dots and ropes of clay.

3. Bake 20 minutes. Add a ribbon for a necklace, or glue on a pin back with E-6000 glue.

Western Wear

Ornaments

- HOW MUCH CLAY?: 1/8 block
- BAKE: 15 minutes / 275°

Roll out a flat sheet of clay—green for cactus, tan for boot. Cut out the shape you want— use a cookie cutter, or cut your own pattern. Press spine marks into the cactus with a toothpick. Decorate the boot with thin ropes of contrast colors. Before baking, poke a hole for hanging.

B★A★D★G★E

- HOW MUCH CLAY? 1/4 block
- BAKE: 20 minutes / 275°

Roll out a flat sheet of red clay and cut out a star with a cookie cutter. Flatten small gold balls of clay and press them onto the points of the star. Use a toothpick to poke a dotted border all around the edge of the star. Cut a small star out of a flat circle of gold clay and press it in place. Before baking, carve the word "SHERIFF" with a toothpick, then highlight with gold paint after baking.

Bandana Slide

- HOW MUCH CLAY? 1/8 block
- BAKE: 15 minutes / 275°

Roll out a flat piece of brown clay and cut out a teepee shape. Press stake lines into the top with a toothpick, and decorate with thin ropes of contrast colors. Roll a rope of brown clay and join the ends to make a circle. Press firmly onto the back of the teepee.

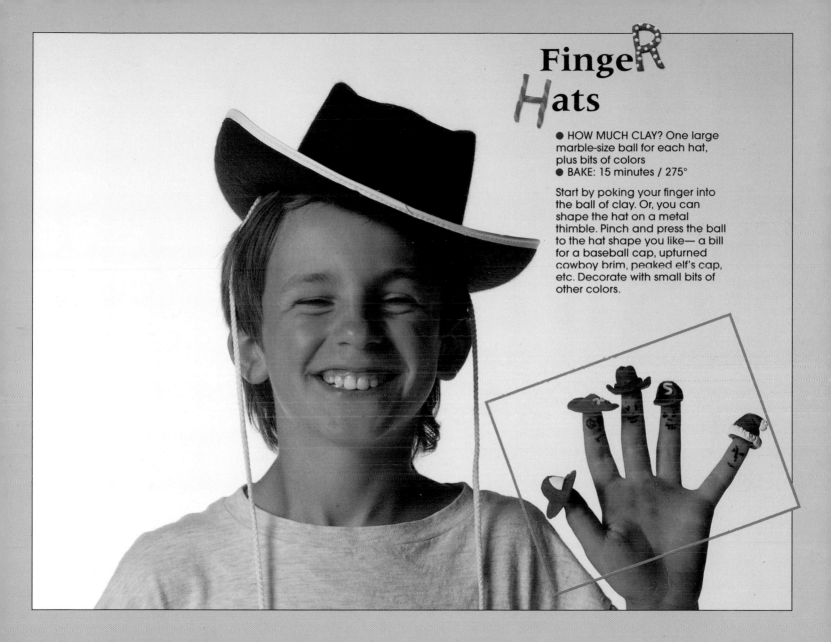

FingeR Hats

- HOW MUCH CLAY? One large marble-size ball for each hat, plus bits of colors
- BAKE: 15 minutes / 275°

Start by poking your finger into the ball of clay. Or, you can shape the hat on a metal thimble. Pinch and press the ball to the hat shape you like— a bill for a baseball cap, upturned cowboy brim, peaked elf's cap, etc. Decorate with small bits of other colors.

Fancy Jars

Mouse Chase

- HOW MUCH CLAY? 1/2 block of purple
- BAKE: 25 minutes / 275°

Cover jar lid with purple clay. Press decorative metal buttons into the top. Make sure they're oven-proof material! Decorate the edge by poking a pattern with a toothpick.

Spooky Hand

- HOW MUCH CLAY? 1/2 block of green for hand, 1/2 block of purple for base, 1/4 block of white, bits of black
- BAKE: 30 minutes / 275°

Cover metal jar lid with purple clay. For hand, make a green rectangle and cut three slits into it for fingers. Round and shape them with your fingers. Mark knuckles with a knife or toothpick. Add fingernails. Stick a skinny rope onto the base of each nail for cuticle. Stick hand on jar lid and bend fingers around the edge. Make a flat white sheet for the cuff and a flattened ball for a button, then

Gone Fishing

- HOW MUCH CLAY? 1/2 block of green plus bits of colors
- BAKE: 25 minutes / 275°

Cover jar lid with green clay. Add a lake-shaped sheet of blue for water. Use brown to make a boat shape and form person with logs and balls. Add a toothpick fishing pole. Decorate the edge of the lid with simple fish shapes. After baking, you can tie a thread on the fishing pole and anchor it in the lake with a tiny dot of glue.

This design is a
circle in the center
with triangles cut and
placed all around it.

The Nicest Jar Lid
You Ever Saw

● HOW MUCH CLAY? 1 block
of basic color, plus small
pieces of other colors
● BAKE: 20 minutes / 275°

Start with a *metal*
jar lid. Roll out a
large sheet of clay. Place
the sheet over the lid
and trim. Then decorate
with shapes of clay and
bake right on the lid.

Tooth Fairy Tooth Holder

● HOW MUCH CLAY? A large marble-size ball
● BAKE: 15-20 minutes / 275°

Make a plain pot: Flatten the bottom of a ball of clay, stick your finger down into the top of the ball and shape the edge around your finger. Flatten a ball for the lid. Make letters from thin ropes and attach them to the pot with a toothpick. To make the tooth, start with a teardrop of white clay. Slit the skinny end to form two "legs." Press the edge of a toothpick all along the top of the tooth, use tiny black dots for eyes and a rope for a mouth. Stick onto the lid. Bake pot and lid separately.

Pot with Coiled Lid

- HOW MUCH CLAY? 1/4 block
- BAKE: 15-20 minutes / 275°

1. Take a ball of brown clay and flatten the bottom by pressing it down against the table top.

2. Poke your finger down into the middle of the ball and hollow out the inside. Be sure to leave some bottom.

3. For the lid, make a rope and a tiny ball.

4. Coil up the rope and top it off with the ball. Bake.

Flower Pot

- HOW MUCH CLAY? 1/2 block total
- BAKE: 20 minutes / 275°

1. Mix red and brown for a nice terra cotta color.

2. Roll out a long rectangle.

3. Bend the rectangle into a cylinder shape and press the seam together.

4. Roll out a long snake and press it around the top of the pot.

5. Flatten a ball and pinch it until it is slightly larger than the base of the pot.

6. Set the pot on top of the disk base and bake.

Since baked clay is waterproof, you can fill your pot with soil and plant a live plant in it.

Basket

- HOW MUCH CLAY? 1/4 to 1/3 block
- BAKE: 20 minutes / 275°

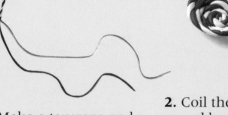

1. Make a tan rope and a brown rope, then twist them together as shown.

2. Coil the twist into a round basket, gradually building up height with each turn.

To make it easier to shape the basket, cover the bottom of a glass jar with a piece of foil and wind the twist around it. Gently remove the jar and bake the basket. After it cools, peel the foil out.

Spiral Bowl

- HOW MUCH CLAY? 1/4 to 1/3 block
- BAKE: 20 minutes / 275°

Roll two long skinny ropes, one red, one white, and twist them together. Flatten a red ball into a circle for the base of the bowl. Wrap the twist once around the flat circle and attach it by gently smoothing the seam with your finger. Coil the twist around, making a slightly bigger coil each time.

● HOW MUCH CLAY? 1 block
of light blue clay, 1/4 block
each of red, blue and white,
bits of orange and yellow
● BAKE: 25 minutes / 275°

**Put Yourself
in the
Picture
Frame**

Don't forget a
flower on the hat!

For base, roll out
a large rectangle
of light blue.

Hair is orange clay
pushed through a
clean garlic press.
Wash press
afterwards!

Cut a round circle
where the face
should go.

Bow tie is two red triangles
with an extra piece for a
knot. Decorate tie with
tiny white dots.

Stick figure pieces are
cut from flat rolled clay—
arms, legs, shoes, hat
and gloves.

After baking
and cooling
the frame, glue
a photo behind
it so face shows
through the
cut-out.

Stripes are skinny
white ropes.

Twist red and white ropes
together and wrap
around the edges of
the rectangle.

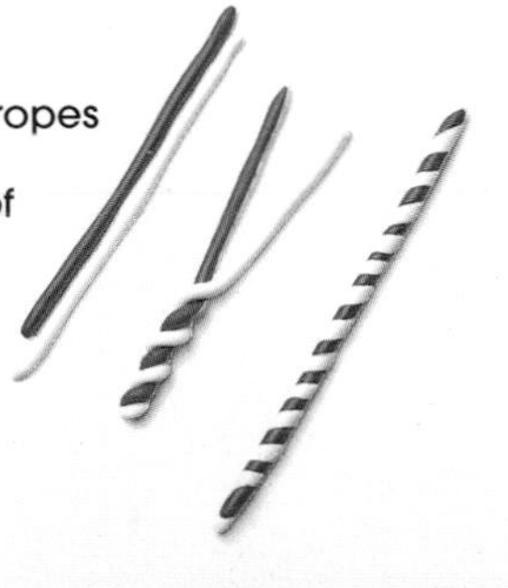

Basic Bead Tips

To make a neat hole in your bead, push a toothpick (or blunt needle) through the bead until you see a little bump on the opposite side. Pull the toothpick or needle out and poke it in through the little bump.

1. Poke with a toothpick until a bump appears on the opposite side.

2. Poke toothpick into bump and out other side.

To keep round beads from flattening on one side as they bake, have your grown-up assistant cut and strighten a wire coat hanger. Thread your beads onto the wire, then balance the wire on the rim of your baking dish as shown so the suspended beads don't touch the bottom of the pan.

Simple Beads

This necklace is made from three simple beads shapes: round red balls, blue balls flattened into fat disks and a yellow log cut into short pieces.

Turquoise Beads

● HOW MUCH CLAY?
Necklace: 1 block of clay
Bracelet: 1/2 block of clay
● BAKE: 10 minutes / 275°
on a wire

Make irregular wedges of
green or light blue clay to
imitate chunks of turquoise.
Pierce them with a toothpick,
then bake them.

You'll need to make a lot of
beads if you want a long
necklace.

For a south-
western bracelet,
we strung some
turquoise
beads with a
few store-
bought
silver ones
on a piece
of elastic
string.

Polka Dot Beads

- HOW MUCH CLAY? 1/4 block for a bracelet
- BAKE: 10 minutes / 275°

1. For a spotted yellow bead, make a yellow ball and several tiny balls of other colors.

2. Lightly press the colored dots onto the yellow ball.

3. Roll the ball gently to smooth it.

4. Poke a hole through the bead with a toothpick.

5. Bake the beads on a wire over the baking dish.

String your beads on elastic string for an easy-on, easy-off bracelet.

Spiral Beads

You can wrap a swirl around a log of clay to make a cylinder bead.

● HOW MUCH CLAY: Small marble-size ball for each bead.
● BAKE: 10 minutes / 275° on a wire

1. Make some plain beads the size of small marbles.

2. Take two contrasting colors and roll thin ropes, then twist the two ropes together as shown. You'll get a spiral stripe.

3. Wrap the rope like a snake around the bead.

4. Roll the bead gently to smooth.

Marble Beads

- HOW MUCH CLAY? Use small marble-size balls for each bead. Size varies.
- BAKE: 10 minutes / 275°

Marble beads are a lot easier to make than they look. Here's how:

1. Make two ropes of contrasting colors and twist them together as shown.

2. Start smushing the twist until the colors start to streak together. Stop when you like the way it looks. The longer you smush, the finer the streaks will get. But don't OVERsmush or the colors will blend together completely!

3. Break off a piece and roll it into a ball.

4. Poke a hole through the bead.

5. Bake on a wire over a baking pan.

Square, Odd, & Un-round Beads

Try other shapes besides round beads. You can roll your ball into a slightly elongated oval, or flatten your ball into a disk. For a doughnut, punch a pencil hole through the center of your disk. You can also roll your clay into a log and slice it into cylinders.

wire

For a fancy coil bead, take your marble twist and coil it like a cinnamon roll. Poke a hole in the top and insert a small wire. Twist the ends of the wire together and push into a round bead. Pierce the round bead and bake the entire thing on a wire for 10 – 15 minutes / 275°.

Take your marble twist and coil it like a cinnamon roll.

Never throw away your used bits of clay. You can smush them together to make marble beads. Don't be afraid to mix more than two colors.

Millefiori Beads

Beads made with repeating patterns or flower designs are called "millefiori," from an Italian word meaning "thousand flowers." These beads are made to resemble the Venetian glass beads that were made in ancient times and used for trade around the world.

A "cane" is a hidden design that runs all the way through a log of clay. You can see the design only by cutting slices off the log. It's like the ring pattern inside a log. You only see it when you slice it.

The Big Cane Secret

The first step to making millefiori beads is always the same: Make a log. Even though you want small beads, the log you make can be pretty fat (sort of like your thumb).

Then, once you've made a fat, fancy log, with a fancy cane inside, you can roll it on a table. The log will lengthen, and the design inside will get beautifully small.

Striped Beads

- HOW MUCH CLAY? Varies. 1/4 block for a short necklace
- BAKE: 10 minutes / 275°

Use any colors you like. We used blue, green and white here.

1. Make a white log as thick as your finger, and a bunch of thinner ropes of blue, green and white.

2. Cut the thin ropes to the same length as the thick log.

3. Place the ropes all around the white log.

4. Roll the log to the width you like, maybe pencil-thin?

5. Cut the log into cylinder-shaped beads.

6. Poke holes in the beads with a toothpick.

7. Bake on a wire. Be sure the beads can slide around on it.

The Sharp Knife and Fridge Secret

Before you cut your cane log into slices, chill it for 30 minutes in the fridge. (Patience!) Then, ask your grown-up assistant to use a sharp knife to cut the slices. A dull knife, or a warm log, will squish too much.

We made fancier beads by pressing flower cane slices (page 72) onto our striped beads, then rolling gently to smooth them.

Cinnamon Roll Beads

1. Roll out two rectangles of contrasting colors. Trim both rectangles to the same size.

2. Stack the rectangles one on top of the other, and roll them up into a cane log.

3. Roll the cane log to the thickness you want, then chill it.

4. Cut chilled thin slices off the log. Use a grown-up equipped with sharp knife.

5. Roll a new log out of a solid color.

6. Place the slices (from your old log) all around the new log.

7. Roll the log so the slices flatten onto it. Then chill it.

8. Cut the log into cylinder beads. (Grown-up and sharp knife required.)

9. Poke holes in your beads then bake them on a wire. Make sure they slide along it. Bake 10 minutes at 275°.

ROUND BEADS

● HOW MUCH CLAY? To start, a large marble-size ball for each color.
● BAKE: 10 minutes on a wire / 275°.

These are like cinnamon roll beads, but they're shaped like little balls, not little logs.

Make a cane and slice it up following steps 1 through 4 on page 68. Then, instead of making a new log, make some solid color round balls.

Place slices all over each ball as shown, then roll gently to flatten the slices.

Pierce the beads and bake them on a wire as usual.

GRRR

Blue and White Lace Beads

1. Roll a white log about pinky-thick. Roll a flat sheet of blue and trim it to the same length as the log.

2. Wrap the blue around the white log.

3. Roll the log into a long rope. Cut the rope into five sections.

4. Stack the five sections into a bundle.

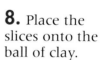

5. Roll the whole bundle into a log of the desired thickness.

6. Cut thin slices off the log.

7. Roll a ball of blue clay.

8. Place the slices onto the ball of clay.

9. Roll the ball between your palms to smooth it.

10. Pierce the bead and bake it on a wire, 10 minutes at 275°.

A Bouquet of Bracelets

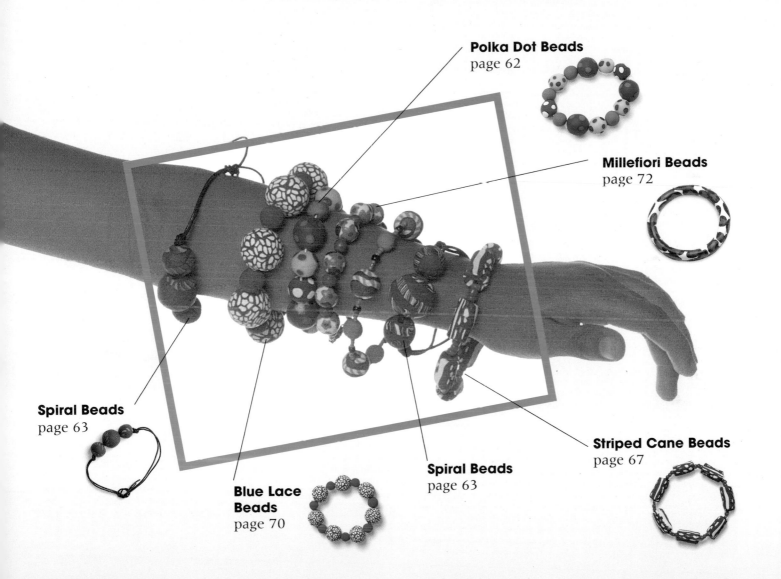

Polka Dot Beads
page 62

Millefiori Beads
page 72

Spiral Beads
page 63

Blue Lace Beads
page 70

Spiral Beads
page 63

Striped Cane Beads
page 67

Fancy Millefiori Beads

● HOW MUCH CLAY? All colors —
a small marble-size ball of each color.
● BAKE: 15 minutes on a wire / 275°.

1. Roll seven skinny logs of equal length: one log for the center, three logs of a different color, and three logs of a third color.

2. Roll out a rectangle slab to wrap the bundle.

3. Place the six contrasting logs around the center log, alternating colors.

4. Wrap the rectangle around the bundle. If necessary, trim ends for an even fit. Now you have a cane log.

5. Roll the cane log to the thickness you want. Chill it in the refrigerator.

6. Cut thin slices off the end of the log.

7. Make a round ball out of a solid color of clay.

8. Next, scatter the cane slices on the ball.

9. Roll the ball gently so the slices flatten onto the ball.

10. Let the bead sit a while to firm up. Then poke a hole through the bead and bake it on a wire.

Millefiori
SHEET

● **HOW MUCH CLAY?** Small balls of colors to make cane. Larger size for slab.
● **BAKE:** 15 minutes / 275°

Hint: Good project for leftover canes — use many different designs together.

1. Make a cane log following the directions on page 72. Chill it in the refrigerator.

2. Roll out a solid color sheet of clay.

3. Cut thin slices off the cane log.

4. Place the slices on the sheet of clay.

5. Cover the clay with a piece of waxed paper and roll over it with a rolling pin.

6. Use a cookie cutter to cut out shapes.

7. Bake the shapes then use them for pins, pendants or decorations.

H·E·A·R·T
R·O·C·K·S

You can use your millefiori canes to make a heart rock. After you've made your cane and chilled it, cut thin slices and place them all over a good-sized bead of solid color. Roll it gently to flatten the slices. Shape the ball into a heart by pinching the bottom and pressing a toothpick against the top center. Before baking, poke a hole as shown for a cord. You can make matching earrings from smaller hearts (start with two same-size balls). For pierced earrings, insert the wires before baking.

● HOW MUCH CLAY? A large marble-size ball.
● BAKE: 15 minutes / 275°

GHOST BEADS

The ultimate cane technique. Putting a picture inside a log is where art and beadmaking truly overlap. Professionals create incredibly elaborate beads using this technique, which we illustrate here with a simple (but charming!) ghost. Once you've learned the basics of this style, you'll be a bead artist.

● HOW MUCH CLAY? 1/4 block each of white and black
● BAKE: 10 minutes / 275°

1. Make a paper pattern by tracing our ghost at far right.

2. Roll out a slab of white clay at least 1/2" thick.

3. Place the ghost pattern on the clay and trace around it with a toothpick. Cut along the line with a paring knife. Smooth the rough edges with your fingers or a toothpick.

4. Use a toothpick to poke holes for the eyes and mouth. Work the toothpick in a circular motion until the hole is big enough to fill with black clay.

1/2" thick

5. Put your ghost in the freezer for about 20 minutes, until VERY firm. (This will make it a lot easier to place the eyes and mouth.)

6. Roll a thin rope of black clay; make sure the rope is narrow enough to go through the eye and mouth holes. Poke the rope into the holes, using a toothpick to pack the clay in until the holes are completely filled.

7. Surround the ghost with pieces of black clay to fit snugly around the ghost's edges. Make sure that all the black clay is the same thickness as the ghost, 1/2."

8. Trim around the black clay to make a round circle. Put your circle in the refrigerator for about half an hour to bring the design to uniform firmness.

9. Stand your circle upright and carefully roll its edges, first with your fingers, then between your two hands or on a table. The design will start to lengthen into a log. (The ghost on each end will look weirdly distorted—this is normal. The end pieces of a cane usually don't hold the design very well.)

10. When your roll is the desired thickness, let it rest for several hours or put it in the fridge to firm up. Then slice off pieces of the log, using a very sharp blade. (Kids, here's where you need your grown-up assistant.)

11. Poke a hole side to side through each bead and bake.

Ghost Necklace is made by stringing ghost beads together with striped beads made just like the ones on page 67.

Trace me.

Buttons are like flattened beads, which is why we've put them here in the book. We've listed the styles from the simplest to the trickiest, so choose accordingly. Clay buttons are pretty fragile. Dry cleaning will kill them, and a tumble dryer is risky. Regular washing machines are OK.

Buttons

● HOW MUCH CLAY? All buttons require small marbles of clay.
● BAKE: 10 minutes for small buttons, 15 minutes for large / 275°

COIL

Make two ropes of contrasting colors and twist them together. Roll the twist into a smooth striped rope. (If you want a marble effect, keep rolling until the colors start to streak together.) Coil the rope up like a cinnamon roll. Poke holes and bake.

SUNFLOWER

Roll out a sheet of yellow clay and cut out flower shape. Flatten a small brown ball and press it into the center of the flower. Poke holes and bake.

LADYBUG

Flatten a red oval and press the center line with a toothpick. Add a small black oval for the head and some tiny black dots. Poke holes and bake.

TWO-TONE BUTTON

Flatten a dark blue ball for the base. Flatten a light blue ball and cut a snowflake shape by cutting small triangles from all around the edge, and a star shape from the middle. Press the snowflake gently onto the base. Poke holes and bake.

BLUE BUTTON

Flatten a blue ball into a circle. Use a toothpick to lightly prick a pattern into the button. Poke holes with a toothpick, then bake.

ROUND FLOWER BUTTON

This is a cane design. Start with a purple log in the center, then wrap it with a slab of turquoise. Lay five yellow and five green ropes all around it, then wrap the whole thing with a slab of red. Roll the cane log and chill it. Cut 1/8" slices from the cane log. Poke holes in the slices, then bake them.

SUN

Roll out a sheet of yellow clay and cut out sun shape. Stack tiny squashed balls of black and white for eyes and shape a red mouth. Poke holes and bake.

FLAG HEART

Roll red and white ropes and lay them side by side. Cover them with a sheet of waxed paper, then roll them out with a rolling pin. Remove the waxed paper and cut out heart shapes. Press a thin piece of dark blue into one corner. Cut out a few tiny stars and press them in place. Poke holes with a toothpick, then bake.

STRIPED BUTTON

Lay ropes of different colors side by side, cover with waxed paper, and roll out with a rolling pin. Cut out circles, poke holes and bake.

ORANGE & GREEN BUTTON

This is a cane, just like the beads on page 72. Make a fat orange log, twelve green ropes and twelve skinny yellow ropes. Place the yellow and green ropes all around the orange log. Roll the cane log to the button diameter, then chill it. When it is firm, slice button-thick pieces from the end of the log. Roll a thin green rope and cut it into short pieces to lay across the buttons. Poke holes and bake.

Cinnamon Square Buttons

● HOW MUCH CLAY? A large
marble-size ball of each color
● BAKE: 10 minutes / 275°

1. Roll out two rectangles
of contrasting colors and
trim them to the same
size.

2. Stack the rectangles one
on top of the other, then
roll them up like a
jellyroll.

3. Roll the cane log long
enough to be cut into four
equal pieces.

4. Stack the four sections
as shown.

5. Use a rolling pin to
flatten all four sides. Roll
just a little on the top,
then flip the clay one
quarter turn. Keep this up
around all four sides until
you have
a nice
smooth
square
loaf.

6. Put the loaf in the
refrigerator to
firm it up.

7. Cut the loaf into 1/8"
slices.

8. Poke button holes
with a toothpick,
then bake.

All Kinds of Pendants

Ice Cream Pendant

Use your finger to roughen the surface of a small ball of clay to look like a scoop of your favorite flavor. Make a tan cone, press a waffle pattern with a toothpick and stick the cone and scoop together. Poke a hole through the scoop then bake 10 minutes. Thread onto a thin satin ribbon.

Disk Pendant

The disk is made by shaping a doughnut out of a round piece of clay. Roll out a slab of clay and cut out a circle, then cut a smaller circle out of it. Use a blunt end of a pen cap or end of an eraser to texture all over to look like pounded metal. Bake 10 minutes. To give an antique look, apply acrylic paint then wipe it off. Loop a leather cord through the pendant. If you like, add a couple of swirl beads.

Belt Loop Arrowhead

- HOW MUCH CLAY? Large marble-size ball of gray
- BAKE: 20 minutes / 275°

1. To form into arrowhead shape, make a diamond shape and pinch around the edges to resemble a sharpened flint.

2. Poke a large hole in the top for hanging.

3. Bake.

4. Loop a leather cord through the hole to hang on belt loop.

Snake Pendant

Curve a rope into a squiggly snake, curling the tail back into a loop. Add a tiny red rope mouth and flattened white balls for eyes. Bake 10 minutes. For a necklace, tie a thin ribbon or cord through the tail loop.

Knot Pins

● **HOW MUCH CLAY?**
Small marble-size ball of each color.
● **BAKE:** 15 minutes 275°

Roll ropes of contrast colors and twist them into a fancy knot. Bake. Glue on a pin back with E-6000 glue.

These rings are variations of the ones on page 41.

Heart Chokers

1. Roll out a flat sheet of clay and cut out a heart shape.

2. Decorate the heart with glass gems or with dots and ropes of colored clay.

3. Insert a metal jewelry ring into the top of the heart, then bake 15 minutes at 275°.

4. String on a black velvet cord.

Trace me.

Holiday Pins

Tree

● HOW MUCH CLAY? One large marble-size ball of clay.
● BAKE: 15 minutes / 275°

1. Roll out a flat green sheet and cut out a tree shape.

2. Decorate with glass gems or colored bits of clay.

3. Press a pin fitting onto the back, and hold it in place with a thin piece of clay. Bake.

4. If you like, you can embellish with glitter glue after baking.

White ball for hat pompom.

Flat red triangle for the hat.

Flatten a pink ball for the face.

Santa

● HOW MUCH CLAY? One large marble-size ball plus small bits
● BAKE: 15 minutes / 275°

Red ball for holly berry. Pinch two holly leaves out of green clay and press veins with a toothpick.

Flat white strip for the hat band.

Nose and eyes are tiny balls.

Add white beard and moustache.

Candy Cane Earrings

Roll thin ropes of red and and white and twist them together to make a striped rope. Bend rope into a cane shape. Make holly from bits of clay and stick on. Insert eye pin into top, then bake 10 minutes at 275°. Hang on ear wire.

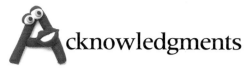

Acknowledgments

Special thanks to Nan Roche, Barbara Morrison, Ellen Gadberry, Pamela Dueweke, Kay Hohbach of Monkeyshine Clothing, Tanya White, Brooke Rovig, Michelle Gearig, Kevin, Alan and Jessica Erdmann, George Hofmann, Shirley Hofmann, David Edwards, Dan Haab and John Torres.

And thanks to the kids and grown-ups who lent us their smiling faces, hands and feet: Casey Weiss, Nicky Weiss, Brennyn Torres, Georgia Rae Rosenberg, Katie Rosenberg, Joe McAndrew, Molly McAndrew, Mihir Kshirsagar, Colin Gooding, Davey Franco, Kaela Fox, Peter Fox, Susan Fox, Siobhan Feehan, Nicole Davis, Anne Cheever and Jacqueline Cheever.